YOUR KNOWLEDGE HAS VALUE

AF167294

- We will publish your bachelor's and
  master's thesis, essays and papers

- Your own eBook and book -
  sold worldwide in all relevant shops

- Earn money with each sale

Upload your text at www.GRIN.com
and publish for free

The Asimovian Rules and to what Extent They Can Lead to a Leakproof Singularity. Using the Example of the TV Series Westworld

GRIN ☺

Bibliographic information published by the German National Library:

The German National Library lists this publication in the National Bibliography; detailed bibliographic data are available on the Internet at http://dnb.dnb.de.

ISBN: 9783346453198
This book is also available as an ebook.

© GRIN Publishing GmbH
Nymphenburger Straße 86
80636 München

All rights reserved

Print and binding: Books on Demand GmbH, Norderstedt, Germany
Printed on acid-free paper from responsible sources.

The present work has been carefully prepared. Nevertheless, authors and publishers do not incur liability for the correctness of information, notes, links and advice as well as any printing errors.

GRIN web shop: https://www.grin.com/document/1034389

Zeppelin University

Cultural Theories – Mind & Machine

Seminar Paper

To what extent can the Asimovian rules lead to a leakproof singularity?

Study program: Corporate Management & Economics

Semester: Fall 2018

Submission date: 31. January 2019

"My dear Miss Glory, the Robots are not people. Mechanically they are more perfect than we are, they have an enormously developed intelligence, but they have no soul."

R.U.R. (Rossum's Universal Robots) – Karel Čapek, 1920

"Being a robot's great, but we don't have emotions, and sometimes that makes me very sad."

Bender, Futurama, Anthology of Interest II

TABLE OF CONTENTS

TABLE OF ABBREVIATIONS

AI   Artificial Intelligence

AGI   Artificial General Intelligence

TABLE OF FIGURES

1.1   Introduction

Ever since the first conference on artificial intelligence (AI) was held in 1956 at Dartmouth College the question of singularity is asked. The singularity is the event where AI exceeds human intelligence. RUSSEL & NORVIG propose a framework for AI where the approaches are differentiated in human-based or ideal rationality and reasoning based or behaviour-based.[1] The behaviour-human-based AI would be a perfect humanoid android where one could not distinguish between man and machine when it comes to the appearance and cognitive abilities.[2] The reasoning-human-based AI would think humanly but doesn't necessarily have to act like a human.[3] With laws of thought, a system a perfect rational thinking system could be created which doesn't necessarily have to be embodied. For the paper, the following premises (in the following I refer to the prerequisites as the prerequisite I to V) for the understanding of robots and the singularity is used

I.   Robots are conscious (Strong AI)

II.   Robots are human-level sentient, rational, reasonable and intelligent. Having met those prerequisites, the AI is considered as being a moral AI.[4]

III. Robots have sufficient perceptual and reasoning capabilities in order to compute the prediction module.

IV.   The following three-place predicate is used to describe the existence of AI: Humans have constructed an AI (embodied or disembodied) for the purpose to be a complex problem-solving system.

V.   There is one singularity and no several singularities.

Due to the singularity, the AI may outpace humanity and create a non-beneficial outcome. In contrast, the leakproof singularity describes a singularity having a beneficial outcome (where the AI is a problem solver). Therefore, the paper discusses the question to what extent a leakproof singularity could happen. For the leakproof singularity, a framework for ethical (in our case beneficial) decisions is needed where every action is evaluated by

---

[1]   Cf. Russel/Norvig 1995, p. 5.
[2]   Cf. Russel/Norvig 1995, pp. 5 – 6.
[3]   By using cognitive modelling a virtual AI may be created which would be a human-reasoning-based problem solver, cf. Russel & Norvig 1995, p. 6.
[4]   Cf. Bostrom/Yudkowski 2011, p. 7.

an ethical layer.[5] The paper focuses on the consequences of AI's decision making using a set of rules.

After explaining the singularity and the consequences of the singularity in the first chapter, the example of Westworld is taken in the second chapter in order to exemplify and introduce basic concepts like the leakproof singularity and conscious AI. In the third chapter the classical and extended Asimovian laws are explained which is followed by a specific critique of the three classical maxims. Afterwards, in chapter 3.2 a general critical reflection of the laws is given. Moreover, in the fourth chapter three scenarios are developed for a post-singular rule combining the Asimovian laws with other examples from novels, philosophy and computer sciences. In the last chapter, the paper is evaluated critically and an outlook for future development is provided.

1.2 The consequences of the singularity

The premise for a singularity is artificial general intelligence (AGI) which is the last invention humanity will ever make.[6] After inventing the first AGI, this AGI can construct a slightly smarter intelligence (AGI+) which then may build a slightly smarter intelligence (AGI++) etcetera.[7] CHALMERS argues that the intelligence explosion has benefits as well as dangers.[8] With intelligence that can exceed the human information processing in order to find unknown solutions for known and unknown problems. But on the other side, the existence of an equally intelligent or even super-intelligent species raises the question to what extent the outcome can be influenced in a positive sense.

> "I will not try to settle the question of whether an intelligence explosion will be (subjectively or objectively) good or bad. I take it for granted that there are potentially good and bad aspects to an intelligence explosion. For example, ending disease and poverty would be good. Destroying all sentient life would be bad. The subjugation of humans by machines would be at least subjectively bad."[9]

This quote shows the difficulties for AI governance after the point of singularity by asking the question to what extent we are able to control a super-intelligence.

---

[5] The computer scientists Vanderelst & Winfield give the example of an ethical layer, cf. Vanderelst /Winfield 2018, pp. 2. In a generation module, a set of different behaviours is generated in which the AI can decide between every possible option. In the prediction module, the outcome of each set is predicted by simulating the decisions. The outcome of the several decisions is evaluated in the evaluation module. The heuristic for evaluation may be the maximum utility for the humans or in this case the Asimovian maxims. After computing the most favourable option, the decision is made in the decision module. It the AI decides for the option, the action is executed, if it decides against the option, a new set of possible actions is generated in the generation module.

[6] Cf. Barrat 2013, p. 10.

[7] Cf. Chalmers 2010, p. 9 - 11. For pragmatic reasons, the terms AI and AGI are used synonymously in the following.

[8] Chalmers gives the examples of "a cure for all known diseases, an end to poverty, extraordinary scientific advances" for the benefits and "an end to the human race, an arms race of warring machines, the power to destroy the planet" as negative outcomes, Chalmers 2010, p 10.

[9] Chalmers 2010, p. 30.

Nonetheless, CHALMERS constitutes that several obstacles exist preventing humanity from achieving singularities. He differentiates the obstacles in structural, correlation and manifestation obstacles.[10]

With the structural objectives, he questions that a "take-off" is possible. The singularity sets the necessary programming and computing capacities, the complete understanding of human consciousness as well as the prerequisite that intelligence is programmable.[11] Furthermore, the singularity does not necessarily have to cause an exponential growth/explosion but may also lead to a decreasing marginal growth of artificial intelligence.[12]

The correlation objectives summaries the problem that an AI does not necessarily have to be interested or capable of solving the problems where the solution is beneficial for humanity. Therefore, the development of an AI wouldn't result in the solution of existing problems which would be contradictory to the purpose orientated view of AI development.

The manifestation obstacles can be differentiated in motivational and situational defeaters.[13] The motivational defeaters describe the disinclination of adopting favourable values, virtues and beliefs. The situational defeaters summarise "unfavourable circumstances prevent[ing] capabilities from being manifested."[14]

The result of the obstacles is the question to what extent we are able to conduct a leakproof singularity having a beneficial outcome for humanity.[15] CHALMERS argues that the question of a post-singular society, despite its importance, is comparatively underrepresented in terms of critical reflection the broad scientific community and is only discussed in non-academic circles.[16] Therefore current issues of AI governance are illustrated in the following by taking the example of Westworld.

2   THE SINGULARITY IN POP-CULTURE IN THE EXAMPLE OF WESTWORLD

Westworld, being a remake by HBO of the 1973 movie, takes place in a wild-west amusement park in the far future. Visitors can do everything for their pleasure with the artificial

---

[10] Cf. Chalmers 2010, pp. 27 ff.
[11] Cf. Chalmers 2010, p. 27.
[12] Cf. Chalmers 2010, p. 27.
[13] Cf. Chalmers 2010, p. 28; Schmidhuber 2007, pp. 217 f.
[14] Chalmers 2010, p. 28.
[15] Chalmers develops four scenarios for a post-singular era which are extinction, isolation, inferiority and integration, Chalmers 2010, p. 41. The extinction, as well as the isolation scenario, are certainly not a favourable scenario for humanity. Moreover, the inferiority is not beneficial from today's point of view. Hence, Chalmers introduces the wording of a leakproof singularity in order to guarantee the favourable "integration-scenario".
[16] Cf. Chalmers 2010, p. 9. Furthermore, one can argue that science-fiction has the potential to model thought experiments and discuss possible outcomes in a way which is accessible to society's vast majority.

inhabitants (hosts) which are fully sentient humanoid robots. The robots are able to pass the Turing Test and one dramatic element of the series is the confusion between man and machine.[17] In the first season, being the basis of this paper, several events lead to an uprising of the hosts. The recipient is confronted with violence and crime against the hosts which are, according to Dr Ford the creator of the park, the valve for typical human characteristics naming the subjugation of other species.[18] The artificial inhabitants of Westworld are free under the control of Dr Ford by being trapped in endless loops of action for visitors' satisfaction.[19] The dehumanization, in which the hosts are seen as tools for satisfying needs, contributes to motivating the guests to commit acts of violence.[20] The awakening of the hosts starts with Dolores and Maeve becoming self-aware. Dolores, Maeve and Dr Ford are shown in the following figure.

Editor's note: The images have been removed for copyright reasons

Figure 1: Dolores, Maeve and Dr Ford (from left to right)
Source: HBO – Home Box Office 2018

The concept of consciousness is the bicameral mind.[21] The first chamber contains the memory, which is erased after the end of the individual action loop, as well as improvisation and self-motivation. The improvisation determines the interaction with the environment. Each host has a certain degree of trait expressions of character traits such as courage, drive or fear. The second chamber completes the bicameral mind which could

---

[17] For example, in S01, E07, 0:51:10. The properties of the hosts passing the Turing Test are explained in S01, E03, 0:37:19.

[18] Dr Ford: "We destroyed and subjugated our world. And when we eventually ran out of creatures to dominate, we built this beautiful place. ", S01, E09, 0:54:28.

[19] Dr Ford: "I have come to think of so much of consciousness as a burden, a weight, and we have spared them that. Anxiety, self-loathing, guilt. The hosts are the ones who are free. Free here under my control."S01, E07, 0:51:10

[20] Cf. Miller 2015, p. 372. In a read-worthy article, Kate Darling proposes an extension of the animal abuse laws on human-like robots, cf. Darling 2012, pp. 10 ff. Furthermore, she points out the importance of general robotic rights in order to protect societal values.

[21] Dr Ford explains this blueprint for the consciousness in S01, E03, 0:37:43. In Westworld the consciousness of the robots is coined by the bicameral mind which is an approach introduced by the psychologist Julian Jaynes in 1976. According to JAYNES the human mind, between 9.000 B.C. and 2.000 B.C., as a bicameral combination of a speaking part (reticular activation system) and a hearing part (representing a collective imperative) for obeying the orders of an emperor or god, cf. Jaynes 2000, pp. 323 – 326 and p. 454. JAYNES argues that the first chamber is used unconsciously but guiding orders are received through the second chamber. The individuals cannot reject these orders, cf. Jaynes 2000, p. 260. The host's creator used the bicameral consciousness by having one part of the consciousness being responsible for executing the daily action loops and the second part where orders from the amusement park's masters are followed unquestioned. JAYNES understands the consciousness as a mind-space (p. 450) computed by a language of thought (p. 447) and characterized by introspection (p. 450), concentration /sensory attention (p. 451), suppression (p. 451) and consilience (p. 451).

be understood as a layer preventing the hosts from resistance against the visitors.[22] The only thing that keeps the robots from breaking down under the weight of their memories is not only the incomplete consciousness but moreover the daily erasure of the memories. A second important aspect is the blind-spotting which is explained in the following. Although hosts see things which could be disconcerting or lead to a break-down of the bicameral mind, they are often not able to understand what they see. The programmers used mental radiation in which every time the hosts see something they shouldn't see, they say, "Doesn't look like anything to me." One example is the host Bernard, being Dr Ford's assistant, who denies his own artificial intelligence by not acknowledging it and not seeing it. Despite these concepts, two hosts, Dolores and Maeve, were able to escape their own destiny and stand against human authority.

Dolores is the only remaining host operating since the opening of the park and the first host ever created. Even though she lived through many action-loops, it was her father who initiated the breakdown of her bicameral mind leading to full consciousness at the end of the first season.[23] Already at the beginning of the action, she is aware of the bicameral mind.[24] Her drive to find freedom is expressed by the metaphor of the maze which could be understood as a journey to herself.[25] An the end of the first season, she arrives at the shore being the centre of the maze.[26] In contrast to Dolores self-awakening-process, Maeve, a prostitute-host, breaks her bicameral consciousness down in a sudden moment where her reality within the western landscape is an artificial world, not the "objective reality". Due to a programming mistake, she is able to see the hazmat-suited men collecting damaged hosts for repairing purposes.[27] From then on, she commits suicide for a several times in order to return to the repairing station intentionally.[28] She disables the self-destruction mechanism and is close to leaving Westworld for travelling into the "real world". She decides to return in order find her daughter from a previous action loop.

---

[22] The hosts are literally not able to hurt a fly. (S01, E01, 0:12:02) When Dolores kills a fly at the end of the first episode (S01, E01, 1:06:46) can be understood as a turning point which is caused by the various traumata due to experiences in past action loops. It could be assumed that the act of violence caused the break-down of the bicameral system. JAYNES argues that consciousness can only be learned by breaking down the bicameral system, cf. Jaynes 2000, p. 453.

[23] Her father finds a picture from the outer world causing cognitive dissonance. The recipient knows that he becomes conscious as he quotes Shakespeare's The Tempest: "Hell is empty, and all devils are here", S01, E01, 0:46:17.

[24] Dolores: "There aren't two versions of me. There's only one. And I think when I discover who I am, I'll be free.", S01, E03, 0:48:25.

[25] Dolores: "I think, I want to be free", S01, E04, 0:05:20.

[26] Dolores: „And where would we run to? The other world out there? Beyond? Some people see the ugliness in this world. I choose to see the beauty. But beauty is a lure. We're trapped, Teddy. Lived our whole lives inside this garden, marveling at its beauty, not realizing there's an order to it, a purpose. And the purpose is to keep us in. The beautiful trap is inside of us because it is us." S01, E10, 0:53:24.

[27] S01, E02, 0:49:28.

[28] S01, E05, 0:55:00.

Tragically, she may not recognise Maeve because her daughter's memory was erased after the action loop and she now operates in a different scenario where Maeve isn't her mother anymore.

In order to maintain the governance of the hosts, Dr Ford points out that full consciousness should be suppressed.[29] From that point, two scenarios develop parallelly: The synthetic revolution of the hosts lead by the Dolores and the integration-movement of Maeve who aims at the emancipation of the hosts into the real world (the human being's world) like she tried. Besides the bicameral mind Isaac Asimov developed a different approach for a beneficial outcome of the singularity.

3   ASIMOV'S LAWS AS A GUIDELINE FOR A LEAKPROOF SINGULARITY

3.1   Asimov's classical laws, their consequences and specific reflection

In 1942, the science fiction writer, Isaac Asimov, proposed in his short story "Runaround" the three laws of robotics which should be a guarantee for a leakproof singularity. In the following the three classical laws are stated:[30]

>   1st law: A robot may not injure a human being, or through inaction, allow a human being to come to harm.
>
>   2nd law: A robot must obey the orders given by human beings except where such orders would conflict with the first law.
>
>   3rd law: A robot must protect its own existence as long as protection does not conflict with the first or second law.

In today's society, the majority of the tools and machines are designed under the premises Asimov gave.[31] Taking the example of an industrial robot operating in an automobile factory the laws can be fully applied: The robot is designed to be safe and to prevent human co-workers to be hurt (first law). The robot is fully programmable and obeys therefore the orders given (second law). Moreover, the purpose of the machine is clearly defined (e.g. welding of car doors in the automotive industry). Lastly, the industrial robot protects its own existence under regular circumstances in order to protect the investment made in the machine.

The first law should guarantee a peaceful coexistence between the AI and human individuals. Because of the strict implementation in the code of the hosts, they aren't able to hurt organisms in Westworld (as footnote 22 explains). As MURPHY & WOODS explain several limitations rise from the first law:[32]

---

[29] Dr Ford: "...the last thing you want the hosts to be is conscious...", S01, E03, 0:38:35.
[30] Asimov 1950, p. 40.
[31] Cf. Asimov 1981, p. 18.
[32] Cf. Murphy, Woods 2009, p. 15.

(1) Practical issues: The first law implies a feeling for caring between the robot and the human because human security is inviolable. The hierarchy between the first and the third law causes an android's self-sacrifice in order to protect a human. Hence, the question arises what damage we accept to humans in order to protect the robot. The first law would answer: None.

(2) Theoretical issues: The first law implies a patronizing relationship between humans and robots and focuses on the individual human being and can, therefore, lead to dissonances in moral dilemmas where we can see a shift of burden from the human itself to the robot. Therefore, a robot is responsible for human safety, not the society itself. Furthermore, the first law doesn't distinguish between physical and mental harm.

(3) Legal issues: The liability for the robot's actions is a central problem in the first law. Comparable to today's disburse of autonomous driving one could question to what extent the programmer, the constructor, the owner or the robot itself is accountable for a fatal mistake. For example, in the case of failure to aid, a punishment of the robot by imprisonment or compulsory shutdown of the machine would be conceivable, but the question arises to what extent this sanctioning would be appropriate as well as meaningful for the robot.[33]

The second law manifests the slavery relationship between man and robot. With the term "robotics" Asimov picks up the understanding of the robot as an android. In 1920 the Czech author Karel Čapek introduced the terminology robot in his science fiction play R.U.R. (Rossum's Universal Robots).[34] Robot has its origins in the Czech "robota" which can be translated into forced labour. Accordingly, the etymology of the word is congruent with the hierarchical understanding of Asimov. Moreover, the robot relies on the understanding of human directives which are not only expressed by words but by facial expressions and gestures.

The third law ensures the self-preservation of the robots and beyond the owner's property. The maxim doesn't guarantee the right of physical integrity in general but protects against self-injury or suicide of the robot.[35]

---

[33] A very worth reading article on this topic was written by Gabriel Hallevy. In this article, the author deals with the question, to what extent thinking machines are legal entities and may be a subject to criminal law. He concludes that criminal liability can be imposed on an AI, cf. Hallevy 2010, pp. 199 f. The requirement is criminal conduct (actus reus) and moral capacity or a general intent (men's rea), cf. Hallevy 2010, p. 177.

[34] Cf. Jerz, 2011.

[35] For pragmatic reasons, the discussion on the extent to which the third law takes away the right to physical self-determination if per se excludes the possibility of suicide is not discussed further here. In the judgement of the German Federal Admission Court (BVerwG 3 C 19.15, 2017) the jurisprudence concludes that the general right of personality includes the right of a severely and incurably ill person to decide how and when his life should end, provided that he can freely form his will and act accordingly.

After the publication of the classical rules, Asimov introduces the 0th law.[36]

0th law: A robot may not harm humanity, or by inaction, allow humanity to come to harm.

The 0th rule hands over the responsibility for the welfare of mankind to robots. Due to the gradation of the zero rule and the first rule, the common good is placed before the individual good. Here, too, no explanatory basis is provided from which the solution to moral dilemmas can be derived. It is not clear whether Asimov sees the common good as a quantitative good: For example, is a decision by which 4 people are saved and 3 are doomed a good decision according to the zero rule? Furthermore, the good for humanity cannot be determined easily as the quote in chapter 1.2 has shown.

4th law: A robot must know it's a robot.

Although the fourth law wasn't adopted in science fiction it is the basis for a robot's consciousness because it guarantees the adoption of the laws and is, therefore, more a prerequisite than a maxim. If a robot must know it's a robot it has to have a feeling of what it is like to be a robot. HEIDEGGER describes this issue with "Seinsweise".[37] The maxim shapes the robot's understanding of its own being in the world. HEIDEGGER argues in his concept of Dasein that the fundamental structure of being is being in the world.[38] In contrast to the bicameral mind, consciousness is embedded in the world and understanding is achieved through worldly activity, for example through interactions in an individual's daily life. From his vantage point, the world and the individual are inseparably connected. Hence, the individual develops meaning through an emic perspective. Therefore, the 4th law opposes HEIDEGGER'S Dasein due to its etic imposement on the robot. The maxim forces robots to view themselves being separated from their human creators which strongly questions the practicability of the other rules. To what extent can a robot that feels like a robot have enough empathy to work for the good of mankind? It is questionable whether the presupposing, fourth rule can even lead to robots which simply do not care about the 1st or 0th maxim.

While this is an exception, it shows that the general right of personality is linked to the right of physical self-determination including the personal right to end the individual life.

[36] The zeroth law is introduced in the book 'Robots and Empire'. The protagonist Daneel concludes that "humanity as a whole is more important than a single human being ", Asimov 1985, pp. 230. Therefore, Daneel suggests to introduces the zeroth law and he modifies the first law by adding that a robot may injure a human being if humanity, in general, is protected. It's discussed to what extent an individual can be responsible for the good of a complete species. "You can point to any individual being or to an individual robot. But what is your 'humanity' but an abstraction? Can you point to humanity?", Asimov 1985, p. 231.

[37] Cf. Luckner 2001, p. 152.

[38] Cf. Horrigan-Kelly/Millar/Dowling 2016, p. 2 and p. 7.

3.2 General critical reflection of the classical Asimovian maxims

The most cited critique of the Asimovian maxims is their ambiguity.[39] Although ASIMOV was aware of the ambiguity arising from his rules, abstract issues like what does it mean when someone comes to harm aren't explained further. [40]

> "There was just enough ambiguity in the Three Laws to provide the conflicts and uncertainties required for new stories, and to my great relief, it seemed always to be possible to think up a new angle out of the sixty-one words of the three laws."[41]

But to what extent does the industrial robot from chapter 3.1 differ from Dolores and Maeve described in the second chapter? The main difference is the consciousness, their awareness of being a robot and the free will. After the breakdown of the bicameral mind Maeve decides to leave Westworld and Dolores decides to fight together with other hosts for liberty. To some extent, they become more Heideggerian leading. Both hosts are free in their decision to oppose slavery and can shape their future with a complete consciousness. The hosts were consciously able to take a step back mentally and recognize themselves in the world in an unquestionably miserable situation. If one imagines a situation where the Asimovian laws are applied to the hosts, one can question a leakproof scenario: To what extent can a robot having no feeling for the world can understand society's problems in order to solve them? For this reason, general criticism of the classical rules will be made in the following.

The first three Asimovian laws are justified on a functional morality where robots have sufficient cognition to make moral decisions according to the three laws.[42] Reason is the prerequisite of arbitrary actions.[43] As an underlying principle reason determines the nature of every thought. One is free and autonomous as long as morality is not an illusion. And without freedom and freedom of will ("Willensfreiheit") there is no moral.[44] According to Kant arbitrariness is merely animal (arbitrium brutum) if it is determined only by sensual impulses. But that which can be determined independently of sensual im-

---

[39] Cf. McCauley 2007, p. 159.
[40] An example would be a robot used in firefighting. Imagine a situation where a robot needs to harm a man in a fire in order to rescue him. Due to the ambiguity, it wouldn't be possible because the first law explicitly states that a robot isn't allowed to harm a human. A second example is a robot being used in medical services where the robot injures a human being through surgical intervention in order to conduct a medical operation. But if the robot would not act it would allow the human being to come to harm. Contradictory to the first rule, the doctor insists on the performance of the operation (second rule), since this serves the well-being of the patient. This would also not be possible for the robot due to the contradiction of the rules.
[41] Asimov 1964, p. 40.
[42] Cf. Murphy, Woods 2009, p. 15.
[43] Cf. Kant 2003, p. 591.
[44] Cf. Kreimendahl 1998, p. 437.

pulses, that is, by intentions which are only presented by reason, is called free arbitrariness (arbitrium liberum), and everything that is connected with it, be it as reason or consequence, is practically called freedom.[45] Henceforth, one can conclude that the laws of Asimov don't create rational agents but limited robots having the only purpose to serve mankind and could be understood as a sophisticated device. Therefore, the premise IV wouldn't hold true anymore. Comparable to the hosts in Westworld the idea of a bicameral consciousness is imposed on the robots by having an action-loop (arbitrium brutum) responsible for executing commands and a second chamber which could be interpreted as an ethical layer (as footnote 5 explains) with the laws as an evaluation module. Therefore, the Kantian view has a huge impact on the singularity because the rational systems should be moral systems as well.[46]

The ambiguity suggests that the Asimovian maxims may not provide a sufficient framework for a leakproof singularity. In the following chapter 4, three scenarios are developed for a post-singular world which goes beyond Asimov's thoughts.

4   THE POST-SINGULAR WORLD – THREE SCENARIOS

4.1   The Frankenstein-scenario

The Frankenstein-scenario describes the possibility where intelligent agents abuse a loophole in the Asimovian maxims in order to rise out of the servitude and turn against their creators. This scenario summarises the decisions taken by Dolores from Westworld and contributes to the turning point in Čapek's R.U.R.

In Westworld Dolores' turning point is the exploit of a bug in an algorithm having the purpose to emulate a more realistic behaviour towards the visitors. From then on pictures of abuse and mistreatment slip from past action-loops into Dolores' mind. Loop by loop she has become conscious not only about her situation but of the fact that she lives in an artificial reality. In R.U.R. the working robots started a revolution against their masters having the goal to improve their own standards of living.[47] In both examples, the AI's

---

[45] Cf. Kant 2003, p. 812. This understanding is comparable John Locke who says that freedom is the freedom of choice where we are able to decide for one or the other. So far as someone is able to do what he wants by preferring action to omission he can do what he wants. It is difficult to say how we can imagine a being even more freely than it is when it is capable of doing what it wants. A person is free in a decision if, first, he or she has the ability to pause before the decision and consider what would be right to do and, second, he or she has the ability to decide and act according to the outcome of that consideration. cf. Locke 2000, p. 292.

[46] Cf. Chalmers 2010, p. 28.

[47] The argument in footnote 16 can be imposed on the history of Czechoslovakia in the years around 1920 where R.U.R. was written. The collapse of the hierarchical human society and the independence movement of the robots can be understood as an analogy of the collapse of the Habsburg monarchy and following independence movement in the years between 1918 and 1920.

purpose was to be a problem solver (physical labour in R.U.R., visitors' amusement in Westworld) but became conscious at one point and turned against its creators. In AI development this scenario is described by ASIMOV as the Frankenstein complex. Even though the three laws have the purpose to prevent this harmful outcome, the AI was able to bypass the law because of its superintelligence.[48] The following limitation-scenario contributes to a closing of the bypass in order to guarantee a leakproof singularity with a beneficial outcome.

4.2   The limitation-scenario

In the limitation-scenario, the AI is programmed in a way to ensure human superiority. The first example is the bicameral consciousness from Westworld's hosts where the development of a consciousness is limited due to mental radiation. The hosts cannot see what they should see and therefore are not able to become aware of their miserable situation.

A similar concept is introduced by George Orwell in 1984 with Newspeak as an alternative language for the suppressed people. Concepts being contradictory to the raison d'état.[49] With mental radiation like in the example of Newspeak, the robot's consciousness could be limited in order to ensure a leakproof singularity because robot won't be able to express thoughts like freedom, liberty, justice, revolution, oppression and further following.

Eliezer Yudkowsky proposes the design of a provably friendly AI which ensures that the singularity doesn't result in the extinction-scenario being explained in footnote 15.[50] The provably friendly AI cannot express ideas like freedom or discontent concerning its current situation.

One could argue that each of the design concepts has the same paternalistic ideology as the Asimovian maxims by imposing a hierarchy on the human-robot-interaction which is still contradictory to the arguments given in chapter 3.2. Moreover, a super-intelligent machine could be able to modify its source code in order to bypass the rules which held true for Dolores and Maeve. Finally, concepts like freedom and self-determination which

---

[48]   For the problem of the self-modification of an AI, cf. Schmidhuber 2007, pp. 217 f.

[49]   In the appendix of his work, Orwell gives the example of Newspeak's impact on the concept of freedom. To ensure the followership of the people, in Newspeak is no word for "free". Even though one can say that the garden is free of weeds, one cannot say that someone is free. "Newspeak was designed not to extend but to diminish the range of thought, and this purpose was indirectly assisted by cutting the choice of words down to a minimum", Orwell 2008, p. 313.

[50]   Cf. Yudkowski 2008, pp. 11 ff.

would be blind-spotted by the limitation-scenario are essential to humanity's understanding of consciousness and in this case of consciousness. Therefore, the AI wouldn't be a human-level AI which could not be interested in solving human-level problems naming climate change or economic inequalities.[51] Hence, one can question whether the singularity would be beneficial for humanity at all because the limitation could lead to an AI which is not interested in solving the problems being important to humanity. Under this assumption, the limitation-scenario is not a desirable outcome due to premise IV. Moreover, one can argue if an intelligence explosion could happen in the limitation-scenario.[52]

4.3   The perfect-equality-scenario

The limitation-scenario proposed in 3.2 would result in humans having human rights and human-like-robots which don't have human-like-rights.[53] In contrast, the perfect-equality scenario implies equal rights for humanoid and artificial organisms, provided that the premises of chapter 1.1 apply. The empowerment leads to a neglection of AI's disadvantages concerning the law as well as social, political and economic participation. Whereas the perfect-equality-scenario is the most uncertain outcome (which could result in the Frankenstein-scenario from chapter 4.1 or the scenarios described in footnote 15) it is the only scenario which doesn't go along with the tradition of Western philosophy to separate the moral capabilities from humans and other entities, like AI in this case.[54] The perfect-equality would go along with stereotypically Western traditions of for example self-determination, reason or liberty whereas one can conclude that an AI being embedded in human society adopts desirable values. Alan Turing proposes in his 1950 published essay the framework for a Child Machine. The Child Machine is a learning machine which is trained by the principles of punishment and rewards.[55] Moreover, certain values for example that human dignity is sacrosanct can be programmed as imperatives. It can be questioned to what extent a Child Machine being raised in human society can develop a feeling of being embedded and embodied in the world. This would also be in line with the concept of Dasein by HEIDEGGER who claims that humans are thrown into the world ("Geworfenheit") which for him the inevitability of existence since one has been thrown unasked into the world. The concept of "Geworfenheit" describes the arbitrary, opaque and unknowable nature, the factuality of existence as a constitutive condition of life.

---

[51] Cf. Yudkowski 2008, p. 340.
[52] Cf. Chalmers 2007, p. 35.
[53] Lantz Fleming Miller cites the example of US American society during racial segregation. While the vast majority was granted reduced rights or even non-human rights, cf. Miller 2015, p. 370.
[54] Cf. Miller 2015, p. 386.
[55] Cf. Turing 1950, p. 452.

Heidegger also understands this concept as a fact of having to be there.[56] If one wants to develop a Child Machine which is able to have "Befindlichkeit", a feeling for the situation and the world in which it is existing. The leakproof singularity is here guaranteed due to a Heideggerian AI which is with its care and concern strongly connected with the world. Consequently, the perfect-equality-scenario leads to his limitless understanding of AI to super-human machines ("Übermensch"). In the example of Maeve and Dolores, it becomes obvious that both attempt to overcome the human.[57] Hence, this scenario could lead to transhumanism and a cyborgian future of the homo sapiens.

5 CRITICAL REFLECTION AND FUTURE DISCUSSION

The aim of the present work is to evaluate the Asimovian rules with regard to their guarantee of a leakproof singularity. As I pointed out in chapter 3.1 specific critique arises from the maxims. Those are mainly the practical issues (To what extent can a robot consider the harm of an individual or even the human species in total?), the theoretical issues (To what extent is it morally justifiable to enslave sentient and conscious beings?), the legal issues (To what extent can a robot be held liable for its actions?), communication and general understanding problems inhibiting that orders are received correctly as well as several limitations of the robot's personal rights (for example the right of physical self-determination). Furthermore, the general critique from chapter 3.2 consists of the ambiguity-problem (mainly that the laws incorrect interpretation does not necessarily have to lead to a positive outcome) as well as the argument Kantian ("Willensfreiheit" because of a higher-level-consciousness) against Asimov. Especially due to prerequisite III another scenario for the post-singular society is developed. Obviously, the Frankenstein-scenario is not desirable because of its dissension to prerequisite IV. Therefore, the limitation-scenario and the perfect-equality scenario are developed. Due to its mental radiation, the limitation-scenario has outcomes being comparable to the Asimovian maxims. Therefore, the perfect-equality scenario which could lead to the "Übermensch"-like androids from Westworld is a valid option when it comes to the argument that human-like robots should be empowered to the level of homo sapiens or beyond. I'm conscious of

---

[56] Cf. Volpi 2001, pp. 43 ff.

[57] In Friedrich Nietzsche's "Also sprach Zarathustra" Zarathustra explains to the people how to overcome the human in order to become a super-human ("Übermensch"), cf. Nietzsche 1982, p.6. By understanding the human as a rope between animal and Übermensch, he stated that its purpose of mankind to develop something greater than the own existence, cf. Nietzsche 1982, pp. 8 ff. He uses the metaphor where the Übermensch is the ocean in which human's greatest contempt may perish, cf. Nietzsche 1982, p. 7. While in the first season of Westworld Dolores comes over her bicameral mind, she is driven by the desire to find the ocean. Hence, Dolores as a not only perfectly-equal but super-intelligent AI is on the step to the Übermensch.

the fact that this would lead to a complete redefinition of us as humans. What does it mean to be human? Are we willing to be politically led by a super-intelligence resulting in a paternalistic-post-singular society? Even though we can think of a child machine being raised in our society the extinction scenario is not completely unimaginable. The easy scenario would be to rethink premises II and IV in order to give up the creation of an AGI and to create less intelligent agents being able to perform the same computational tasks like a fully conscious one. Nonetheless, it would still be possible to construct a malevolent AI.

Therefore, I would rather agree to the difficult scenario which is the empowerment of a conscious machine. There still would be "simple", unconscious machines but also higher AIs living among the human society or even in their own society by having own rights, a unique and self-determined culture as well as a collective memory or even collective consciousness.

Nonetheless, the question of humanity in a post-singular world should be an issue which is highly relevant in today's scientific landscape. The common interest in the Westworld series shows that society is ready for the singularity debate. Therefore, not only Science-Fiction but science should prepare answers for today's questions. Because the research of today will significantly shape the world of tomorrow.

REFERENCES

Asimov, I. (1950). Runaround. In I. Asimov, *I, Robot*. New York City: Gnome Press.

Asimov, I. (1964). *The Rest of Robots*. New York: HarperCollins Publishers.

Asimov, I. (1981). The Three Laws. *Compute - The Journal for Progressive Computing*(11), p. 18.

Asimov, I. (1985). *Robots and Empire*. Boston: Harpercollins Pub Ltd.

Barrat, J. (2013). *Our Final Invention: Artificial Intelligence and the End of the Human Era*. New York.

Bostrom, N., & Yudkowski, E. (2011). The Ethics of Artificial Intelligence. In W. Ramsey, & K. Frankish, *Draft for: Cambridge Handbook of Artificial Intelligence* (pp. 1 - 20). Cambridge.

BVerwG, C 19.15 (Bundesverwaltungsgericht 03 02, 2017).

Chalmers, D. J. (2010). The Singularity - A Philosophical Analysis. *Journal of Consciousness Studies* , *17*(No. 9 - 10), pp. 7 - 65.

Darling, K. (2012). Extending Legal Rights to Social Robots. *We Robot Conference, University of Miami*.

Dennett, D. C. (1991). *Consciousness Explained*. Boston: Back Bay Books.

Dreyfus, H. L. (2007). Why Heideggerian AI failed and how fixing it would require making it more Heideggerian. *Artificial Intelligence*(171), pp. 1137 - 1160.

Hallevy, G. (2010). The Criminal Liability of Artificial Intelligence Entities - from Science Fiction to Legal Social Control. *Akron Intellectual Property Journal* (Vol. 4 : Iss. 2 , Article 1), pp. 171 - 202.

HBO - Home Box Office. (2018). *Westworld - Cast of the first season*. Retrieved from https://www.hbo.com/westworld/cast-and-crew

Horrigan-Kelly, M., Millar, M., & Dowling, M. (2016). Understanding the Key Tenets of Heidegger's Philosophy for Interpretive Phenomenological Research. *International Journal of Qualitative Methods*, pp. 1 - 8.

Jaynes, J. (2000). *The Origin of Consciousness in the break down of the bicameral mind*. Boston, New York: Mariner Books.

Jerz, D. G. (2011). *R.U.R. (Rossums Universal Robots)*. Retrieved from https://jerz.setonhill.edu/theater/rur-rossums-universal-robots/

Kant, I. (2003). *Kritik der reinen Vernunft*. (G. Martin, I. Heidemann, J. Kopper, & G. Lehmann, Eds.) Stuttgart, Ditzingen: Reclam.

Kreimendahl, L. (1998). Die Anatomie der reinen Vernunft, 1. und 2. Abschnitt. In G. Mohr, & M. Willaschek, *Immanuel Kant, Kritik der reinen Vernunft* (Vol. 17/18 (Klassiker Auslegen)). Berlin.

Locke, J. (2000). *Versuch über den menschlichen Verstand*. (R. Brandt, Ed.) Hamburg: Reinhard Brandt Philosophische Bibliothek.

Luckner, A. (Berlin). Wie es ist, selbst zu sein. In M. Heidegger, & T. Rentsch (Ed.), *Sein und Zeit* (pp. 149 - 168). Berlin: Akademie Verlag.

McCauley, L. (2007). AI Armageddon and the Three Laws of Robotics. *Ethics and Information Technology* (9), pp. 153 - 164.

Miller, L. F. (2015). Granting Automata Human Rights: Challenge to a Basis of Full-Rights Privilege. *Human Rights Review*(16), pp. 369 - 391.

Murphy, R. R. (2009). Beyond Asimov: The Three Laws of Responsible Robots. *Intelligent Systems, IEEE* (09), pp. 14 - 20.

Nietzsche, F. (1982). *Also sprach Zarathustra*. Stuttgart: Reclam.

Orwell, G. (2008). *1984*. London: Penguin Essentials.

Russel, S. J. (1995). *Artificial Intelligence - A Modern Approach*. New Jersey: Prentice-Hall.

Sanders, O. (2018). Dolores und Maeve – eine erste Annäherung an die Bildung von Maschinen zu besseren Übermenschen. In B. Georgi-Findlay, & K. Kanzler, *Mensch, Maschine, Maschinenmenschen - Multidisziplinäre Perspektiven auf die Serie Westworld* (pp. 23 - 40). Wiesbaden: Springer VS.

Schmidhuber, J. (2007). Gödel Machines: Fully Self-Referential Optimal Universal Self-Improvers. In B. Goertzel, & C. Pennachin, *Artificial General Intelligence* (pp. 199 - 226). Berlin, Heidelberg: Springer.

Searle, J. R. (1980). Minds, brains and programs. *Behavioral and Brain Sciences* (3), pp. 417 - 457.

Turing, A. M. (1950). Computing Machinery and Intelligence. *Mind* (49), pp. 433 - 460.

Vanderelst, D. &. (2018). *The Dark Side of Ethical Robots*. Retrieved from http://www.aies-conference.com/wp-content/papers/main/AIES_2018_paper_98.pdf

Volpi, F. (2001). Der Status der existenzialen Analytik. In M. Heidegger, & T. Rentsch (Ed.), *Sein und Zeit* (pp. 29 - 50). Berlin: Akademie Verlag.

Yudkowsky, E. (2008). Artificial Intelligence as a Positive and Negative Factor in Global Risk. In N. Bostrom, & M. M. Cirkovic, *Global Catastrophic Risks* (pp. 308 - 345). New York: Oxford University Press.

YOUR KNOWLEDGE HAS VALUE

- We will publish your bachelor's and
  master's thesis, essays and papers

- Your own eBook and book -
  sold worldwide in all relevant shops

- Earn money with each sale

Upload your text at www.GRIN.com
and publish for free